SHADOW OF TIME

ANATOLY KUDRYAVITSKY
SHADOW OF TIME

For Paddy –
with all the
best wishes,

[signature]

28/09/07

GOLDSMITH
IRELAND 2005

THE GOLDSMITH PRESS LTD.
Newbridge Co. Kildare Ireland

This book is published with financial assistance from
The Centre for Modern Russian Culture

ISBN 1-870-49113-0

Front cover drawing: Wilhelm Föckersperger
Back cover drawing: Gabriel Zapolyansky

Design Consultant: Martin Connolly
Seen through the Press by Karl Stutz
Printed in Germany

ACKNOWLEDGEMENTS

Acknowledgement is due to the following periodicals and anthologies where some of these poems, or versions of them, first appeared:
Poetry Ireland Review, Cyphers, The SHOp, Riposte, New Muses, Litspeak Dresden, Le Journal des Poetes, Autre Sud, Alora, James McKenna: A Celebration, The Edgeworth Papers Volume VII, Vilenica 2002, Who is Who: Poetry Collection, Europski Glasnik.

The author wishes to express his sincerest gratitude to the following for their support, their advice and their encouragement in literary matters: Ann Leahy, Joanne Limburg, Kieran Furey, Patricia Nolan, Jim Kates, Daniel Weissbort, Geraldine Meade, Alison Maxwell, Helen Khokhlova, Prof. Maria Popova, Tatiana Kudryavitskaya, Dr. Thomas Weber, Tina Delavre, Dr. Annelore Nitschke. Also to Paula Meehan, Macdara Woods, Pat Boran, Dermot Bolger, Cathal Ó Searcaigh, Desmond Egan, Theo Dorgan, Peter Sirr, Joseph Woods, Gerard Reidy, Séan Lysaght, Sheila O'Hagan, Cíaran O'Driscoll, Michael Coady, Philip Casey, Paul Perry, Leland Bardwell, Séamus Hosey, John McNamee, Alan and Fionnuala Dukes, Richard Bruton. To my daughter Julia. To my family in Louisburgh and Westport, Co. Mayo; especially to Kathleen Kitterick.

In memory of my aunt
ISABEL KITTERICK
1932 - 1989

CONTENTS

Deer Watch Glaciers Receding

Where images
merge into imagination
and mossy mosaics of stones become
readable like a book of days

we stand and speak about Eros of erosion
and the remote final iciness
we fancy new pastures and
fields of sand

mud up to our knees
the future is pretty unclear and we
don't know how to nurse our new-born freedom
but we are happy as we can be

who thinks of hecatombs of hunting
and Bambi Reading societies
for millenia
to come?

and even this
can't be worse than
glacé
smiles of boundless glaciers

Hunting in Flagged Vicinities
(For Gail Hazelton)

When you kill wolves
people die

it is always the case

they bury the corpses
together with the wolves

long after
they exhume them
and re-bury them wrapped in flags

each time they take the flags
from the living

the latter squat
and cry a lot
naked
shielding with both hands
not what naked people usually shield

but some spots of wild greyish wolfskin
on their breasts and withers

Visitors' Book

Around the corner of a blind lane
in the maze of my inner vision
there is a dusty room and a guest
standing at the threshold.

'Write briefly,' he repeats,
'Give it only a slight press.
I am a Visitors' Book, and
everyone leaves his trace.'

I sit him down in an arm-chair
that looks like a reading-desk.
I offer him
a glass of wine.

'Weak ink,' he squeaks
after taking a sip,
'Come on,
engrave your words.'

I am being very careful,
I don't use sharp instruments,
but there is blood on my fingers
and the inscription is not visible.

The Book of Meros

Papyrus recently found
in the desert of unthinkable
stripped the profession of chronicler
of all covers of sense.

At the very top of the scroll
a few words can be seen
set down in a very shaky handwriting:
The Book of Meros.
It is believed to be
the title of the manuscript.

Down the endless glossy coils
riders gallop, chariots whirl,
swords clink, buildings collapse.
No one sits there
making sense from a past.

The roll absorbs everything that happened
since the dawn of creation
up to the movable 'now'.
With each passing day
The Book of Meros is getting longer
but the memory of generations
is getting shorter.

The march of events will soon
catch up with the flow of time
and then, possibly, overtake it.
Who knows, maybe this means
that we shall read in the mornings
of what we are destined to do
throughout the day.

What shall we do
after we learn what we'll do:
that is the question.

The Golem of Arbour Hill

He appears from behind Collins Barracks,
the acromegalic giant.
His empty eye-sockets contain
medieval gloom,
his pale Celtic skin
fits tightly his stubborn Viking chin.

He strides heavily
along the miry lane of desire
flushing slow birds and
tapping out pulsation in his head:
If you don't know where you come from,
where can you go?
Those who come along are all the more unable
to locate themselves in space and time
because maps are muddy and calendars
have no dates for days like this.

Plunged into multiplying visions, he really
has nowhere to go,
except into his own dream.

In that dream, martyrs of evolution
follow the path from Nowhere to Erewhon:
a jawless fish, dinosaur and
anthropoid ape.
They all keep saying in motion:
Nowhere to go,
nowhere to go,
but where they arrived is now known.

Probably, he is drifting in the same direction
in no hurry to reach there,
unlike hasty pedestrians,
dwellers of the swarming city that repeatedly
thrusts them back to the remote past,

into the times of jawless fishes, dinosaurs
and anthropoid apes.

The Border Mouse

He lives in no man's land.
If a boundary-line is drawn across a river,
he's a fish;
if it cuts through a bog,
he turns into a frog.
All the same, he is
border mouse, mole, moss-trooper.

He gets into carriages at stations,
rummages through bags and trunks and purses,
jumps down through lavatory holes.
Don't worry about him,
he'll come to no harm.

Whether mouse or marmot, he speaks in
the language of Give-Me,
gnaws nets of words
like the roots of a sapling.
Although they have sought him
since the days of old Ur,
no one has caught him.

He demarcated the estates
of King Humpty-Dumpty
and Prince Dumpty-Humpty.
Annulled by edicts,
he annulled those who issued them,
though he more often annulled
very ordinary people, nibbling out
their lamentable lives.
To do him justice, he dug
their graves for them.
The unmarked ones.

One Night in Hamburg
(For Ger Meade)

'Europe is shrinking, but America
is broadening,' the man said,
'We'll all be Americans soon.'

After a glass of schnapps
his red hair stood on end,
thin neck flushed unhealthily.

'Are you Irish?' somebody asked.
'Yeah, I'm Irish. And German as well.
And French, Polish, Swede, everything you like.
I'm out of work at the moment.
Hate to talk about it.'

Somebody topped up his glass to loosen his tongue.

'I am a tester of executions,' he continued.
'I was crucified, hanged, broken on the wheel,
shot, electrocuted, given lethal injections.
They were trying out a humane capital punishment on me.'

'And you are still alive!'

'Pretty much so - if we all are still alive.
But there's no room for me in Europe now.'

And he walked out into the black,
almost African, Hamburg night.

Pseudoaluminium and the Big Plans

The bigger the house,
the smaller the occupants of the house.

The same goes for the devil:
in huts he used to oust the inhabitants,
while in skyscrapers he can go into a snuff-box.

The devil gradually loses prestige.
His dung, however, still lies in the fields.

They send students
to investigate this red clay.
They hope, it contains much
pseudoaluminium,
the raw material of super-high-speed bombers
and portrait frames.

Polluters of Void

And then come
the cleansers of void,
these pellucid flies
sweeping words
with a bubbling vacuum inside,
advising us now against using 'o'
when we make a speech.

Look, over there, where a newspaper flies
flapping wings
and names run
shedding sounds on the way,
closely pursued by a chap with a paunch
who is wielding a brush.

But where should we look?
They have all disappeared,
gone off the air
for the last time,
polluters of void,
denizens of oblivion.

Europe in the Mirror of my Teapot

is hard to recognize: this silvery curve
enlarges France and Germany
but lessens other states

Ireland is barely visible
Russia tends to slide away
to the dark side of existence

all the gaps between capes and islands
are mended
as if an invisible giant put in stitches

Croatia reaches for Italy
Sweden clings to Denmark
former mortal enemies give each other

hugs of love
maybe it was like that
in prehistoric times

this teapot seems to have its own vision
of the world
and the map of Europe on the wall

practically speaking
teapots serve another purpose
sipping my Bewleys tea

I wonder if I can see the meaning
in this image of unity and distortion
and also their strange synchrony

Talleyrand, or a Good European

Born, like myself, in '54,
he seemed to be in no hurry to cross
the border of the New Era
as he had something to do in old times.

His main gift was
the art of whispering.
His whisper was distinct as a snake hiss
and none the less unambiguous.
It froze air into fear.
It inspired whirlwinds.

Drawn by the hurricane,
armies and palaces moved around the continent,
views and ideas got mixed up.
Later they settled down
forming into new patterns of sand
on the bottom of reason.

He took interest in
remote consequences of splendour:
barbarians inheriting Rome,
bureaucrats taking up the threads after Napoleon -
those ants labouring in elephant's footsteps.

He knew that Europe had always been
breathing the dust of consequences.
He cherished that dust
and collected it.

Doubtlessly, he foresaw United Europe
because it is easy to foresee things
if you live beyond time.
Perhaps, that was why he served
all the European monarchs simultaneously
not without deriving benefit from it.

Pastures of Elderly Men
North Co. Sligo

Exposed to a hypothetical
counting eye in the sky,
sheep twenty-two
and sheep twenty-three
show off the red numbers on their backs.

In shed-like houses
human spare parts are
growing old and gradually
fading into rust.

Sleeves of time smell of dampness.
Fungi-impregnated walls
reminisce about the good old days
of barn dancing
when the earth would call to sky hornpipes
for a tune.

No couples are up for a dance now.

'Women don't survive here,'
a woman of eighty said.

Louisburgh in the Shining of the Famine Time
(For Kathleen Kitterick)

Here among the wistful hills
a leafy sheen of sunlight sails
along the slopes
speaking to silence
in its own language

on the deserted beach
shaded by cypresses
and the brushwood of rhododendron
ghostly figures wait
for their ghost-ship

they will vanish soon
float away to Americay
taking with them
their shiny dreams
and starvation rations of words

as for us
nothing else left but
to watch eternity
breaking up
into human splinters

Shadow of Time
(For Maighréad and Tríona Ní Dhomhnaill)

All songs -
are like one scream of pain,
all tears -
are like a stream,
and houses, hills and cars
flow away with it,
streets, pines and centuries
run following them
leaving behind only the terror
of a trembling light
amidst the primordial basaltic chaos.

Dreaming while you Shave

'A bad hairdresser
cuts everyone's hair close to the skin,'
my grandmother used to say.

In her times
that was regarded as heresy.
They said,
bad thoughts would stick in the hair.

After school, I worked my way home
through the hair-drifts
into which laid their eggs
the grey-winged hens of Zamoskvorechye
somehow considered to be pigeons.

My grandmother acquired the strange habit
of tearing away the last page of my school compositions.
She assured me that later on I would see:
that's the best way to get them done.

My grandfather often said that she intended
to tear away the last page of his life;
that was why he went away and since
floundered through the side-streets of women's hair.

Unhatched chickens laughed at him
out of their bald eggshells.

The Lenses of Asclepius

The century has started with
the crime of the century.

In the clouds pregnant with leaden rain
a private eye is still looking into the case
through the lacklustre
lenses of Asclepius.

The chief suspects for being
the authors of their pitiful verses,
poets join in a conspiracy of silence.

Pity crawls out of fashion.
Grimaces rejecting any mirror
replace mirrors used to reflecting grimaces.

Chiropractors declare in all the latitudes:
Tomorrow is the end of the world.
Let's die with dignity.

Chiropodists
begin teaching us on the quiet
to reverberate in the looking-glass.

At the crossroad in Inchicore
a ragged old fellow rubs his spectacles
and peers persistently
through the front glasses of passing cars.

'Where have all the faces gone?' he asks
the dusty Dublin wind.

Kids hurl empty plastic bottles at
the last poet
of the age of transparency.

To God Almighty, Personal

They bring him their lives in portions,
leaf by leaf.

To him, it all sounds like prose:
mornings saturated with rain,
entangled talks
and spiteful thoughts at bedtime.
Not many think of him, he notes sadly.

There are sore verses, as well,
some masterly, some not.
As usual, the latter prevail.
He reads them through
until stifling clouds start swirling
in his head.

Forced to take a break,
he drinks blue sky juice
and feasts his eyes on the moon
round as a lamp
or the regal crown on a British stamp.

They fetch more lives
marked, 'To Heaven' or
'To God Almighty, personal'.
He has already ordered
thousands of cardboard files
and is sorting out lives.
Successful ones are few,
many are unread.

This is the way he works on his
Selected Stories.

Arithmetic

One of two letters that I write
will be answered,
and one of four e-mails.
One of eight friends
will give me a ring
instead of waiting for me to do it,
and one of sixteen friends
will invite me to visit.
One girl out of thirty-two
will pay me attention,
and one out of sixty-four
will care.
I shall like
one of a hundred and twenty-eight girls,
but she won't be the one who cares.
One man out of two hundred and fifty-six
will agree with me that human relations
are rather hopeless.
He will turn out the sort of person
to whom I'll wish never to relate.

To Florence

Your thoughts
on my mind

your words
on my lips

writing to you
about you
in your own handwriting

Open Book

If the Future sends us Cimmerian messages
this picture must be one of them

under the dark crumbling sky -
a second-hand bookshop that sells
not books but the authors -
speaking dolls

this one -
recounting twenty historical novels
by heart

and that one -
reciting three volumes of his poems

in the candlelit window
Cinderella dances with wooden
Marie Corelli
three daughters of success narrate
the story of their porcelain marriage
to Mr. Nutcracker

I can see my pen-and-ink self
quietly getting onto a shelf

I expect to be selling well -
one can clearly read on my face
the promise of long hours running
filled by incessant intellectual activity

Reacaire
from Derricke's 'Image of Irelande'

It was always like this:
the reciting poet lost in his verse;
the accompanying harpist lost in his tune
with his cheek well pressed to the frame.
The others each doing his own thing:
the dog gnawing on a bone;
the servant warming water in the hearth;
the noblemen seeming to listen,
though one is testing the blade of his sword,
another is checking to see who passes by,
and a third is lost in his thoughts.
Almost every word is wasted on them,
though the fourth one is all ears.

All that remains by the next day
is some throwaway line
and a dim impression of melody
and the inexplicable feeling
that the day was not spent in vain.

Reacaire: reciter

The Rising Tide

'And here also
the rising tide is lapping
inside of me,

the water of black
and the darkness inside of it
and the stars,

no more than the darkness and the stars.
Doctor, is it that absolute darkness
is threatening me?'

The darkness never threatens,
it waits patiently,
then it devours,

but the stars,
in their remote glamour,
will stay -

even not the brightest ones.

Leviathan Learning to Overcome Time
(For Desmond Egan)

The day was left
dark side up
and the rain was spreading
from Warsaw to Waterloo.

If not for lanterns of reason,
who'd notice Higher Germany above Germany?
the drowsy air crooned
inside the sea-shells of Gothic churches.

The bus I was on
sailed the aqueous Belgian plains
on its way
to the coast.

Somewhere between Newlands Cross
and Kildare town
I woke up beneath the sorrow-coloured
Irish sky

to see a tree
growing inside an empty house
and an ancient mound
crowned by new grass.

That day
I was thinking of
Leviathan
learning to overcome time.

Fathoming

Awakened from an unwilling sleep,
I was told: 'It's time
for your verses.'

I came out of my house
into the depths of future.
Little dragon-fly-winged people
fluttered around,
they expected something of me.

I had great success,
I recited about
my life among humans.

A note was brought to me:
'We hardly understood anything.
But how marvellous it sounds -
this long-forgotten language!'

Ars Poetica

1. Poem about the Poem

In order to write this poem
I used a writing book
    USSR State Standard specification number 13309
a padded chair
    USSR State Standard specification number 16371
an office desk
    USSR State Standard specification number 14511
a roller pen
    made in Taiwan

having more perfect equipment
I could have achieved a better result

2. Poet and Poverty

No one needs a poet

Somebody
sometimes
needs his verse
and buys it
dirt-cheap

3. Complete Works

Volume 1. Withdrawn from sale
Volume 2. Demolished
Volume 3. Lost
Volume 4. Never found
Volume 5. Oral versions of the destroyed
Volume 6. Posthumous

Leafing through a Book Catalogue

Disorientation sets in
when one reads of intense eroticism
in the verse of a woman of seventy
and turns the page to be told
of the deep philosophical musings
of a seventeen-year-old.

It could all be true, I suppose;
or perhaps the lines got transposed?

Harms and the Girl

The girl
liked the poet Harms's verses.
    The girl
became the poet Harms's girlfriend.
    The girl said:
'The poet Harms's verses are the best.'
    Later the girl said:
'The poet Harms is a good poet,
but there are other poets, as well.'
    Later the girl said:
'The poet Harms has a number of good verses.'
    Later the poet Harms remembered:
there are other girls, as well.

The House in Ostozhenka Street

I once had a girlfriend
who never went to the lavatory.
She didn't even know
the exact location of it
in our house.

It was a crazy house in
Ostozhenka Street
with an enormous hole in the stairs
leading to nowhere.
We were stuck in upstairs rooms
and used a fishing-rod
to hook out some food
through the kitchen window.

The house liked Gurdjieff
and fed us off the reel with his
music for distorted piano.

From the blear mirrors often emerged
images of the three girls
I fell in love with in succession
in the kindergarten.
They all had the same name
Marina Popova.

Years later the fourth Marina Popova emerged
in the flesh
in dangerous proximity to me -
and everything went to hell,
possibly through the hole in the stairs.

It was the exact time when the house
schooled me to loyalty.
There was only one chair in there,
and that chair I was inseparable from
and took it with me
wherever I went.

Suspicious Rustling of Sandals

Ages ago all the writers were Greek
and all the Greeks pedestrians.

Since then something has changed.

Phalanxes of motorised authors
advance through the mist of unspoken,
their yellow gazing
pierces uneducated darkness
sowing it with the golden dust
of imaginary worlds.

Good dead writers
are also present, though invisible.
It is rather strange to see familiar eyes
in alien faces.

Everything flows,
philosophers discovered.
Everything spreads,
guards of mental frontiers detected.

They insist that space
is measurable with names
but not with poems or reed-pipe tunes.
They have a weakness for passengers
of uplifting best-sellers
and despise nameless pedestrians
who often get stuck
in syrupy dictionaries.

The Knack of Living

When he, in his late thirties,
found a room on the lower premises,
his watch ticked out his epitaph:
'He had the knack of living'.

The restaurant car that he ran
keeps plying between the past and the present,
but his considerable savings
were not enough to buy him a ticket.

My highly successful half-brother...

Having no knack of living,
I never wanted to set my watch by his.
Why he looked down upon me?

His name is now buried
in the sandbox of time
where invisible fingers count
beads of seconds.

A shadow among the living, I hear
other shadows whisper:
'The knack of living -
how skilfully it kills!'

The Chinese Art of Forgetting

(For Joanne Limburg)

Today I am an aged album.
Somebody took all the photos out of me
because his mind -
a cautious dancer -
preferred not to come down to reality
too often.

They open me
and instantly put me aside.
I feel the warmth
of the woollen table-cloth I lie on,
the brown on the black.
I ask myself if I still have something to lose
in time.

Outside the windows
a narrow-mouthed rickshaw
ricochets along the side-streets of Cambridge
and moves my thoughts
all over the map of forgotten things and faces.

There must be the land
where they give us back
all we lost and wasted,

the land of pink
with two fishes in the wheel
on the State seal.

Maybe it is even possible
to get there,

but who knows if it makes sense
to buy a return ticket.

Bunin: Portrait with the Person Missing

In the mirror behind his back
recent times are floating
red flags and standards of the Cossacks
his reflection is
a hollow silhouette

into the space he left
a man is being squeezed
he can't go in, groans
than manages somehow -

and the framework of parallels and meridians
cracks all over the globe

Under the Very Name

(For Ann Leahy)

In my room there lives
someone else
who says, he is my biography.
Strange as it may seem, I
don't know him from Adam
but apparently he doesn't lie.

Some letters arrive for him -
they should have been addressed to me instead.
He is glad to take the opportunity
to be me.
As for me, I haven't the slightest wish
to be him.
When I tell him about it
he smiles a compassionate smile.

The Remote Control
(For Mary Ryan)

In one of the shadowy worlds
created by my post-television
clear night vision
they handed me on
the remote control
of myself.

It is of no use to me:
in the past I was controlled
by a fiendish state,
and there is no chance
to influence the future
having so little energy.

I switch channels
back and forth.
The remote control
is taken away from me
by my wife,
then by my little daughter.

The Depth of my Silence
(For Michael Lane)

Eternal traveller through the
rooms of my sorrow,
I still occupy some space
in one of them.

It is nearly empty now. The furniture
has been taken away, and my books
are whispering in their boxes.
Within four cardboard walls,
I lie in a sleeping bag on the bare floor
and watch white lilies blossoming out
on the black velvet of night.

Meanwhile, bombs go off in Antrim and Bilbao.
The U.S. President talks of big sticks.
Names go on echoing travels.
Faces of those who want to be right
even if they're wrong
cluster together in my dream.
I am fathoming
the depth of my silence.

The next day I sit in a garden
and hear my silence inside me,
this thickness of waters,
wave after wave
ready to flood this garden,
all the gardens of the world.

The watchman comes up to me saying,
'We are closing.'
Yes, I am leaving
and leaving my silence behind.
Yes, my silence remains.

Tonight there won't be a flood.

Practical Absenteeism

I take lessons in Absence.

'Where were you when the bomb exploded?'
'I was having coffee in the neighbouring quarter.'
'Were you a victim of the hold-up of the train?'
'No, I had alighted at the previous station.'

Oh, it's first-class!

I am still far from it, I must confess.
At present I am training myself to be
an absentee in the land of high hopes.
I have already learnt to pass completely
from the memory of those with short memory.

My favourite trick is being absent in group photographs
as if by chance,
it comes harder to me
not to be present among my associates.

Some day I'll cope with that,
I will succeed in my
perfect and irretrievable absence
for sooner or later everybody achieves it,
everybody experiences it.

Pierrot and a Beam of Light

'A beam of light
pursues me,'
he says and covers his
shyness
with his pale fingers.

'It finds me, always finds me,
even in my room,
even under the blanket.'

His face as white as the paper
on which he writes his elegies.

'The beam of light
and shadows around my eyes.'

'The beam of light,
blackness and silver.'

'The beam of light
pursues me,' he starts it
all over again.
'Yes, pursues me,
and it has a face.'

The Zero Year
(For Macdara Woods)

Children decode every sort of cypher
and instantly forget it.

In this zero year
cyphers are getting disobedient.
Rouleaus of paper covered with writing
unroll and replace streams of water
and strips of carpet.
Enigmatic symbols percolate
under closed doors.

All in vain.
No one
is interested in mysteries of ages
any longer.

In this zero year
life ceases to exist in written form.
Newspapers are yawning
with blanks.
Minds are exposed to
an eternity behind,
an eternity ahead
and the soundless mouse-running
of this imperceptible 'now'.

Missing Children

Walking along the pathway of my
unguided dreams
I met the missing children
whose photos I had seen
in a morning paper.
They were coming in the
opposite direction
wearing green Ireland shirts.

I stopped a red-headed freckled boy.
'Dying isn't painful,' he said.
'You simply realise that you don't have to
feed yourself and your thought anymore.'

Right behind him, a wan
fifteen-year-old girl
toiled along.
She was slender, almost pellucid.

'Are you sure you are going
in the right direction?'
she inquired with a melancholy smile

pointing to the vale of Vanishing Hope,
in the shady sadness of which
she had dwelt before.

Oisín Caught in a Time Warp

after James McKenna's sculpture of the same name

Yes, I see, James,
the many-ton might of your intention,
I understand why the man with the child's head
rides astride the war-horse.

In Ireland there are many like that -
child-headed and indomitable.
They gallop in all-overwhelming flocks,
they collide heads in Belfast and Derry
raising the rustle of sawdust inside their skulls,
knocking down careless passers-by -

and penetrating-eyed children
with adults' heads
look at them out of the windows.

Letters of the Burning Book
(For Asya Shneiderman)

Beyond the once and for all locked wicket
there is not even a Jewish cemetery:
they deigned to call it only
Begräbnisstätte, the place where the dead were buried.
Nevertheless, some tombstones could be seen
lined up along the wall
as if waiting for a burst of machine-gun fire.

But what is facing them
is only a muzzle of a starling-house -
mourners
are provided for them.

These were not murdered with bullets,
it was time that killed them.

Their fellow-tribesman who finds himself
near at hand
has much to recall about the dead,
about the living
who escaped bonfires, pogroms and concentration camps
into the twenty-first century,
about the fact that letters of a burning book
dance in flame not every time
and not every time literally.

A Burial Place in Bosnia

(For Michael E. Berezovsky)

By the skeleton
you can't tell the nationality

by the skull either

you can do it only by the clothes -
if they haven't turned to dust

then comes absolute equality

these seeds
won't bear fruit

Snapshots

1.

In the neon void of
the underground
shears of ascending and descending
escalators
clip out
snaps of pale faces

lives
    lives
        lives
exposed
to my eyes

2.

Himalayan terraces -
are like gigantic stairs:
violet
    lilac
        blue
            purple
                crimson, at last -
but there is already heaven up there

The Sausage Trail

How did I come to be in Frankfurt?

Believe it or not, I ate frankfurters
at every meal.
One could girdle the globe with the sausages
I've stuffed into myself:
frankfurters day by day, year after year,
moving me along the sausage belt,
till it took me to Frankfurt,
the sausage metropolis.

A Practical Solution

The strangest thing
I have seen in my life
was a large poster
by a highway in Byelorussia:
'STOP! SHOOT A WOLF!'

Nearby
there is not a single wolf.
I never carry a gun.
I can't even shoot well enough,
and I am not the only one like this.

But isn't it a curious thing that one starts
thinking over
a practical solution
to the task one faces?

The Crack in the Wall
(For Con Maxwell)

Mind the crack in the wall, they said,
what will you do
if the Atlantic wind whistles through it

or the yellow summer rain flows in
or family warmth leaks out
followed by the blue television fog?

Watch how the crack sucks the grains of time,
how some of them escape
and gather in your eyes.

What if you lose yourself in space
or lose your space
or space is lost upon you?

Wouldn't it be wise to write down
who you are and where you come from -
who knows through what chink his memory goes?

And the sight of escaping spirit may somehow
prevent you from
selling your house.

Standing on a Weir

Once a century
the world is divided
into before and after,
a coffee-coloured smooth surface
and whirls.

The water down there
was also divided
into before and after.
Nobody cared for its opinion,
it was sent to the stones.

Somebody may say,
'I think of the water's torture,
of its sobs and moans.'

Somebody may say,
'And please don't tell me
that it gives us
light and heat!'

The Lake Wind

In the grove of human trees -
criptogamous and phanerogamous -
each branch outlines a face

beneath the reminiscences-of-rain-coloured sky
volunteers are always there for the trees
to water and fertilize them

the volunteers encamp just where the trees are rooted
one can hear small talk from the kitchen
it smells of onion dressing

the television tells empty tents
of conflagrations
of cutting down the Martian woods

inhaling the lake wind
I watch some withering trees that failed to stand
the severe test of somebody's care

and I envy any flying leaf
no matter whether blank
or with letters

To Begin Anew
(For Kate Mulligan-Doherty)

'Sorry, we gave you
a wrong life,' they said
not too apologetically.
'Will you begin anew?'

Why not?

And now I am scrutinizing
the wall-paper coloured wall-paper
in the hall with a palm-sized palm.
There go tailed people covered all over with hair
      without waiting their turn,
there runs a little pack of dogs
followed by crawling Siamese twins.

The night of my life comes.
I am still waiting, I confess,
having a cold snack in the meantime,
thinking over
whether I would rather finish my meal
with a herring's tail
or with a sweet biscuit,
or maybe with both together.

The Society of Freezing Poets

(For Alison Maxwell)

My friend, the Professor of madness,
comes late in the evenings
to take my temperature.

He jots down some figures on his green cuff
deducing a formula of planetary freezing
in the age of global warming.

As for me, I am hardly warmer
than the window pane,
my energy is on the wane.

My friend makes up the fire.
'Only the Moscow girls can warm me up,
even on the phone,' he confesses.

Fragments of a broken looking-glass
reflect a thousand German professors
reciting poems on aspects of decay.

Decay stirs, glinting through the night
past the switched off television
where Caliban fights the Taliban.

Esperanto

In memoriam, my father, one of the pioneers
of the Esperanto movement

In the year the United States of the World
was established
Esperanto was adopted as a world language

they sent their children to the isles
where Esperanto had been in use
long before it was invented

rowing-boats with the children
sailed into the crimson decline of
customary words and meanings

ice floes and Viking ships were floating by
penguins were arguing in French
oars were squeaking in Hiberno-English

the children were scared
the end of the journey
remains a linguistic mystery

did the children succeed
in learning Esperanto?
the author who expresses himself

in the vernacular
knows only one thing for sure:
the world nowadays talks double Dutch

and most of the people
don't even have to
study the language

Clare Island
(For Gerard Reidy)

Everything here to suit tourists:
a castle
legends of pirates
a couple of hotels
etc. etc.
and - not to forget -
the snow on the grass in this July
or rather flocks of white wool in the rain

inspecting the hills with a road engineer
you can take notice of the roads
sinking towards the sea
and slipping from under your feet

because every mainland has its island
and every island has its island
and there's a naked man amidst elks and buffaloes
in the ancient fresco on the church wall

and tourists
- *Europe in ten days* -
inquire about what age
is that picture typical for

Tidal Islands

(For Joan and Kate Newmann)

The stars above
seem not to be so eternal.

What the sea casts out
the sky takes in,
and the bare slimy ground floats into
the misty abyss of emerald dream
like the head of a rising
underwater giant.

The wind brings people.
The people bring stones
and place them between families,
generations,
between themselves and eternity.

The sea doesn't object.
The sea is patient.
At any moment it can cover the borrowed land
with slumbrous waters
but it waits,
the sea waits,
it gives everything a chance.

At night the moon smoothes out wrinkles
on the face of the sea
and trims the water of black
with silver lace.

Those who saw the wedding dress of the sea
rippling by so slowly,
did they ever think,
like I am thinking now,
that we borrow from eternity
everything we see and hear,

we borrow even ourselves -
only to return it all duly,
just as schoolchildren return their compositions,
with all the mistakes they have made -
to be corrected in red ink

Festivities Go On

On public holidays
the warmth of the crowd holds you captive.
You merge into a vast mutual body.
Only your raised hands are free
but have nowhere to go to
except down to the pebbles of heads.
Cigarette smoke searches pockets and lungs.
Your tongue is quite autonomous
but your words get lost
among thousands of other words.

If you doze off
you will see anything in your dream,
even skeletons
marching past through the Red Square
and rockets watching them closely
from the rostra.

When you open your eyes again
festivities will endure.
You'll still have a chance to observe
huge inflated faces
rising lightly into the air.